Forsa Saεiida

Egyptian Arabic for Beginners

By
Soheir Nada

(soheirnada@yahoo.com)

Forsa Saɛiida
Egyptian Colloquial Arabic

iUniverse books may be ordered through booksellers or by contacting:

iUniverse
1663 Liberty Drive
Bloomington, IN 47403
www.iuniverse.com
1-800-Authors (1-800-288-4677)

ISBN: 978-1-4759-1484-9 (sc)
ISBN: 978-1-4759-1485-6 (ebk)

Printed in the United States of America

iUniverse rev. date: 07/18/2012

TABLE OF CONTENTS

Introduction

This book "**Forsa Saɛ iida**" is designed to provide a quick and fast way of learning Egyptian Arabic language with opportunities to practice. It is created to boost learners' confidence in handling day-to-day activities while living in Arabic countries.

The transcription method is used in order to accelerate Egyptian Arabic spoken language performance.

Grammar explanations and drills are included to clarify and facilitate practical use of the language.

The book includes basics life situations such as:

- Exchange basic information: names, countries etc.
- Asking about unknown things
- Telling time
- Ordering Food and Drinks
- Describing Objects and People
- Taking a Taxi and Giving Directions
- Shopping for Vegetables and Fruits

Each lesson includes:

- Pictured Key Words, Main Dialogue, Vocabulary, Grammar, Drills, Real Life Dialogue
- Six Appendices are containing essential terms that have been covered in all lessons, such as Questions Words, Prepositions, Adjectives etc.
- An Arabic- English Glossary and English-Arabic Glossary.

Soheir Nada has been working as an Arabic instructor at the Post Language Program at the U.S. Embassy in Cairo-Egypt since 1989. She participated in developing class materials, preparing special courses for different departments at the Embassy (Political, Economic, Consular section, …etc.), and also preparing and testing American employees for Foreign Service Institute (FSI) tests.

Symbols that used in this book to express letters in Arabic have no equivalent in English:

Symbol	Sound
H	hard and deep "h"
ع	deep "a"
š	sh
x	kh
'	glottal stop
?	glottal stop (originally q in classic Arabic)
gh	french "r" as in "Paris"

Lesson 1

forsa saɛiida !

Nice to Meet You!

Lesson Contents:

1- Greeting words

2- Subject Pronouns (*I, you {m., f.}*)

3- Question Words (*what?*)

4- Possessive Pronouns (*my, your {m., f.}*)

1

Key Words

sabaaH ilxeer   masaa' ilxeer

ana

ana Kareem

inta   inti

inta Tom   inti Dalia

DIALOGUE:

forsa saɛiida ! *(Nice to Meet You!)*

Kareem : sabaaH ilxeer !

Tom : sabaaH innuur !

Kareem : ana ismi Kareem, wi inta ismak eh ?

Tom : ana ismi Tom.

Kareem : forsa saɛiida ya Tom !

Tom : ana asɛad, wi inti ismik eh ?

Dalia : ana ismi Dalia.

Tom : forsa saɛiida ya Dalia !

Vocabulary

sabaaH ilxeer	*good morning*
sabaaH innuur	*good morning (response)*
ana	*I*
ism	*name*
ismi/-ak/-ik	*my name / your name (m., f.)*
wi /wa	*and*
inta/inti	*you (m., f.)*
eh	*what*
forsa saɛiida	*nice to meet you*
ana asɛad	*nice to meet you (response)*

<u>Drill 1</u>: Choose the appropriate response:

1- sabaaH ilxeer !   a- ana Linda.

2- inta ismak eh ?   b- masaa' innuur !

3- forsa saʕiida   c- ana asʕad.

4- ismik eh ?   d- ana ismi Kareem.

5- masaa' ilxeer !   e- sabaaH innuur !

<u>Drill 2</u>: Reorder the words and make a sentence:

1- ismi – ana – AHmad

2- inta – eh – ismak – ?

3- eh – wi – ismik – inti – ?

4- wi – Mike – ismik – inti – ismak – Dalia – inta

4

Grammar:

Greetings

There are two main greetings. We use one in the morning and the other during the afternoon and the evening.

sabaaH ilxeer	*Good morning*
sabaaH innuur	*Good morning (response)*
masaa' ilxeer	*Good evening*
masaa' innuur	*Good evening (response)*
forsa saɛiida	*Nice to meet you*
ana asɛad	*Nice to meet you (response)*

Equational Sentences:

The equational sentences have no verbs because Arabic doesn't use a lexical equivalent for the verb "*to be*" in present tense. These sentences consist of a "Subject: (noun or pronoun)" and a "Predicate: (adjective, noun or phrase)".

- ismi Tom.   *My name is Tom.*

Subject Pronouns

Arabic has two types of pronouns: independent and suffixed. Subject pronouns are the independent pronouns and in this stage we'll introduce 1st and 2nd person (singular):

- Arabic shows a difference in gender in 2nd person singular.

ana   *I*

inta   *you (m.)*

inti   *you (f.)*

- Subject Pronouns serve as subjects of equational sentences:

  - ana Tom.   *I am Tom.*

Question Word

eh   *What?*

* Note that we use the question word "**eh**" at the end of the question.

  - ismak eh ?   *What is your name?*
                         (your name what?)

Possessive Pronouns Suffixes:

Possessive Pronouns (*my, your*) are different than subject pronouns (*I, you*) in Arabic. While subject pronouns are independent, possessive pronouns are suffixed to nouns (they are attached to the end of the noun: "**i**" in "ism**i**").
It is like saying "*name-my*" instead of "*my name*"

Subject Pronoun	ana	inta	inti
Possessive Pronoun	---i	---ak	---ik
ism	ism**i**	ism**ak**	ism**ik**

Drills

Drill 1: Choose the correct possessive pronoun (-i / -ak / -ik):

1- ana ism- … Sara.

2- inta ism-… John ?

3- ana ism-… Mona, wi inta ism-… eh ?

4- inti ism-… Linda.

5- inta ism-… Kareem, wi inti ism-… Salwa.

Drill 2: Translate into Arabic:

1- I am Mona.

2- I am Tarek.

3- Are you Mike?

4- Are you Dalia?

5- My name is Linda.

6- My name is Samiir.

7- Is your name Jack?

8- Is your name Suzy?

9- What is your name (m.)?

10- What is your name (f.)?

11- Nice to meet you.

<u>Drill 3</u>: Form questions for the following:

Ex: ana ismi John. --------   inta ismak eh ?

   1- ana ismi Kareem.
   2- ismi Samiir.
   3- ismi Dalia.
   4- ana ismi Mona.

<u>Drill 4</u>: Translate into English:

   1- inta ismak Moniir ?
   2- ana Mona wi inta ?
   3- inta Tarek ?
   4- forsa saɛiida.
   5- inti ismik eh ?
   6- ana ismi Fariid wi inta ismak Mike wi inti ismik Linda.
   7- sabaaH ilxeer
   8- ana asɛad.

Listening:

Learn: bawwaab: *guard*

     naddaf : *you (m.) clean (imperative)*

     haat li : *you (m.) bring me*

     gornaan : *newspaper*

Listen to the dialogue and answer the questions:

1- Circle any word you recognize.
2- What is the guard's name?
3- What does Mr. Magdi want the guard to do?

Dialogue B:

Magdi   : sabaaH ilxeer !

MaHmoud : sabaaH ilfoll ya beeh.

Magdi   : inta ilbawwaab iggidiid ?

MaHmoud : aywa, ya beeh.

Magdi   : ismak eh ?

MaHmoud : MaHmoud ya beeh.

Magdi   : tayyib ya MaHmoud, naddaf ilɛarabiyya
       di, wi haat li iggornaan.

MaHmoud : ilahraam walla ilaxbaar ya beeh ?

Magdi   : ilahraam ya MaHmoud.

Lesson 2

miin da ?

Who Is That?

Lesson Contents:

1- Greeting Words (more)

2- Object Pronouns *(with preposition* **"bi"***)*

3- Possessive Pronouns *(m., f.)*

4- Gender *(m., f.)*

5- Demonstrative Pronouns *(this and that {m., f.})*

6- Question Words *(who?)*

7- Numbers 1-5

Key words

mas.		**fem.**	
?alam		tarabeez<u>a</u>	
baab		suur<u>a</u>	
beet		ع arabiyy<u>a</u>	
fingaan		kobbaay<u>a</u>	
raagil		sitt	
walad		bint	
kitaab		šant<u>a</u>	
maktab		saaع<u>a</u>	

Key words

ahlan wa sahlan *welcome*

zimiili *my colleague(m.)*   **zimiilti** *my colleague(f.)*

miraati *my wife*
goozi *my husband*

DIALOGUE:

miin da ? *(Who Is That?)*

Kareem : masaa' ilxeer, ya Tom.

Tom : masaa' innuur !, miin da ya Kareem ?

Kareem : da zimiili Fariid.

Tom : ahlan wa sahlan, ya ostaaz Fariid, ana Tom.

Fariid : ahlan biik, ya Tom !, di miraatak ?

Tom : aywa di miraati Linda.

Fariid : ahlan wa sahlan, ya madam Linda !

Linda : ahlan biik.

Vocabulary

masaa' ilxeer	*good evening*
masaa' innuur	*good evening (response)*
miin	*who?*
da/di	*this -that (m., f.)*
zimiili/ zimiilti	*my colleague (m, f.)*
ahlan wa sahlan	*welcome*
ahlan biik/-i	*welcome (response) (m., f.)*
ostaaz /-a	*Mr. - professor (m., f.)*
miraati/ miraatak	*my wife / your wife*
aywa /la'	*yes / no*
madam/ aanesa	*Mrs./ Miss*

14

<u>Drill 1</u>: Answer the questions:

1- miin Fariid ?
2- Fariid zimiil Tom ?
3- Linda miraat *(wife)* miin ?
4- miin gooz *(husband)* Linda ?

<u>Drill 2</u>: Choose the appropriate response:

1- miin da ?	a- di miraati Linda.
2- ahlan wa sahlan !	b- la', di zimiilti Mona.
3- miin di ?	c- da zimiili Fariid.
4- masaa' ilxeer !	d- ahlan biik.
5- di miraatak ?	e- masaa' innuur !

<u>Drill 3</u>: Right or wrong:

1- Linda miraat Kareem.   ( )
2- Kareem zimiil Fariid.   ( )
3- Fariid zimiil Tom.   ( )
4- Linda miraat Tom.   ( )

15

Grammar:

Greetings

ahlan wa sahlan   *welcome*

ahlan biik / biiki   *welcome (m., f.) (response)*

Object Pronouns:(Suffix Pronouns)

The Object Pronouns occur in the form of suffixes attached to prepositions and they are almost the same as possessive pronouns. When the preposition ends with vowel the 2nd person singular (m. and f.) suffix changes as follows: Masculine: "**-ak**" to " **-k** " and Feminine: " **–ik** " to "**–ki** "

	inta	inti
	---k	---ki
(bii)	ahlan bii**k**	ahlan bii**ki**

Question Word

miin   *Who?*

Gender:

All Arabic nouns have gender. They are either masculine or feminine. Generally, feminine nouns end with an "a" sound which is the sound of letter "teh marbuuta" (ة) in the Arabic alphabet; and a noun without a feminine suffix is masculine. The feminine suffix "a" is also used to derive a feminine noun from a masculine one (zimiil – zimiila)

| kitaab (m.) | suur**a** (f.) |

Demonstrative Pronouns

The Arabic demonstrative pronoun, like subject pronouns, shows a distinction in gender.

| da | *this/ that (m.)* |
| di | *this/ that (f.)* |

* To form a sentence, the gender of the demonstrative pronoun has to match the gender of the noun.

da raagil.	*This (m.) is a man.*
da kitaab.	*This (m.) is a book.*
di sitt.	*This (f.) is a woman.*
di suura.	*This (f.) is a picture.*

Possessive Pronouns:

We previously learned that possessive pronouns (*my, your*) are suffixed to nouns (they are attached to the end of the noun: "**i**" in "zimil**i**").

zimiili Fariid.   *My colleague is Fariid.*

Masculine:

Subject Pronoun	ana	inta	inti
Possessive Pronoun	---i	---ak	---ik
zimiil	zimiil**i**	zimiil**ak**	zimiil**ik**

Feminine:

In feminine words we change the feminine suffix "**a** ة" to "**t**" before we add possessive pronouns.

Subject Pronoun	ana	inta	inti
Possessive Pronoun	---i	---ak	---ik
zimiila	zimiil**ti**	zimiil**tak**	zimiil**tik**

• <u>Notes:</u>

The first name rather than the family name is commonly used with titles:

ostaaz Fariid

<u>Numbers:</u>

0- sifr ---------- (٠)

1- waaHid ------(١)

2- itneen --------(٢)

3- talaata--------(٣)

4- arbaɛa--------(٤)

5- xamsa --------(٥)

Drills

Drill 1 : Introduce your colleague:

Example:

- da zimiili Fariid.
-- ahlan wa sahlan ya ostaaz Fariid.

Drill 2 : Answer with "aywa" or " la' ":

Example:

- Tom zimiil Fariid ?
-- la' Kareem zimiil Fariid.

1- Linda miraat Fariid ?
2- Kareem gooz Linda ?
3- Linda zimiilit Fariid ?
4- Fariid zimiil Kareem ?

<u>Drill 3</u>: Give the object pronoun appropriate to the person (k – ki):

1- ahlan bii…. ya AHmad.

2- ahlan bii… ya Mona.

3- ahlan bii… ya madam Kareema.

4- ahlan bii… ya ostaaz Saɛiid.

<u>Drill 4</u>: Translate into English:

1- Mostafa zimiil Fariid.

2- Mona miraat ɛali.

3- Fariid gooz Diina.

4- di zimiiltak ya Fariid ?

5- da goozik ya Nadia ?

6- Mona zimiilit Dalia wi AHmad.

<u>Drill 5</u>: Reorder the words and make a sentence:

1- ya – miin – AHmad – da – ?

2- miraati – di – Mary

3- wa – ya – Fariid – sahlan – ostaaz – ahlan

4- Linda – biiki – ya – ahlan

<u>Drill 6</u>: Provide the correct demonstrative pronouns (da –di):

1- ……… zimiili AHmad.

2- ……… miraati Samiira.

3- ……… madam Nadia.

4- ……… ostaaz Jack.

<u>Drill 7</u>: Put the sign ♀ or ♂ for each noun:

1- kitaab   6- suura

2- beet   7- ?alam

3- saaƐa   8- šanta

4- Ɛarabiyya   9- zimiila

5- zimiil   10- maktab

<u>Drill 8</u>: Make the possessive of the 1st person singular and 2nd person singular (m., f.) out of the nouns in drill 7:

<u>Drill 9</u>: Translate the following into Arabic:

1- my watch

2- your (m.) cup

3- your (f.) house

4- my colleague (f.)

5- your wife

<u>Drill 10:</u> Write the answer in words:

    a)   2 + 3 = ...

    b)   1 + 2 = ...

    c)   4 - 3 = ...

    d)   5 - 1 = ...

<u>Drill 11:</u> Answer the questions:

eh da/di ?

miin da/di ?

23

Listening:

Learn: gamiila /Hilwa : *beautiful*

                      saHba   : *friend (f.)*

                      atkallim   : *I talk*

Listen to the dialogue and answer the questions:

1- Circle any word you recognize.
2- Who is Mona?
3- Who is the beautiful girl?

Dialogue B:

Magdi   : AHmad miin ilbint ilHilwa di ?

AHmad : feen di ?

Magdi   : illi gamb Mona.

AHmad : Mona miin ?

Magdi   : Mona zimiilitna fi ilmaktab.

AHmad : aah ! di saHbit Mona.

Magdi   : di gamiila awi !

AHmad : raayiH feen ya Magdi ?

Magdi   : raayiH atkallim maɛa Mona fi iššoghl.

Lesson 3

izzayyak ?

How Are You?

Lesson Contents:

1- Greeting Words *(hello)*

2- Suffix Pronouns *(how are you {m., f.})*

3- Question Words *(how?)*

4- The verb *"to have"*

5- Adjectives *(good, tired, happy, sad)*

6- Negation *(not)*

7- Numbers 6-10

Key words

mabsuut

mabsuuta

zaʕlaan

zaʕlaana

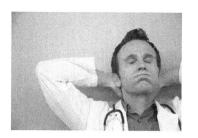

taʕbaan

taʕbaana

DIALOGUE:

izzayyak ? *How Are You?*

Samiira : ahlan ! izzayyak ya Kareem ?

Kareem : kuwayyis awi ilHamdu lillah ! wi inti izzayyik ?

Samiira : miš kuwayyisa, taɛbaana šiwayya.

Kareem : inti taɛbaana walla zaɛlaana ?

Samiira : la' ana miš zaɛlaana, bass ɛandi bard.

Vocabulary

ahlan	*hello*
izzayyak /-ik	*how are you (m., f.)?*
ya	*O, vocative particle*
kuwayyis /-a	*well, good (m., f.)*
awi	*very*
ilHamdu lillah	*God be praised*
miš	*not*
taɛbaan /-a	*tired (m., f.)*
šiwayya	*a little bit, few*
walla	*or*
zaɛlaan /-a	*sad, upset, angry (m., f.)*
bass	*but*
ɛandi/-ak/-ik	*I have/ you have (m.)/ you have (f.)*
bard	*cold*

27

Drill 1: Answer the questions:

1- miin taɛbaan ?

2- Samiira zaɛlaana walla taɛbaana ?

3- miin kuwayyis ?

4- Kariim zaɛlaan ?

Drill 2: Choose the appropriate response:

1- ahlan !   a- ana kuwayyisa awi.

2- izzayyak ?   b- la' ana miš zaɛlaan.

3- inta zaɛlaan ?   c- ahlan !

4- izzayyik ya Mona?   d- ana taɛbaan šiwayya.

Drill 3: Right or wrong:

1- Kareem kuwayyis awi.   (   )

2- Kareem taɛbaan.   (   )

3- Samiira miš kuwayyisa.   (   )

4- Samiira mabsuuta.   (   )

Grammar:

Greetings

ahlan   *hello*

ahlan   *hello (response)*

Vocative Particle

The particle "**ya**" is used before the name or title when we directly addressed a person.

- ya Kareem

Question Word

izzayy   *How?*

Suffix Pronouns:

Subject Pronoun	inta	inti
Suffix Pronoun	---ak	---ik
izzayy	izzayy**ak**	izzayy**ik**

The Verb "to have":

Instead of using a verb to express the concept of "*to have*", the preposition ("*at*" "**ɛand**") + an object pronoun suffix is used (*I have ----- at me*)

Subject Pronoun	ana	inta	Inti
Object Pronoun	---i	---ak	---ik
ɛand	ɛand**i**	ɛand**ak**	ɛand**ik**

Adjectives

Adjectives follow the nouns they modify and agree in gender.

Example:

Tom kuwayyis.   *Tom is good / well.*

Mona kuwayyisa.   *Mona is good /well.*

Masculine	Feminine	
--------	------**a**	
kuwayyis	kuwayyis**a**	*good, well*
taɛbaan	taɛbaan**a**	*tired, not feeling well*
zaɛlaan	zaɛlaan**a**	*sad, upset*
mabsuut	mabsuut**a**	*happy*

Negation:

Equational sentences (no *"to be"* verb) are negated with miš.

- Diina miš kuwayyisa.   *Diina is not well.*

- Kareem miš zaɛlaan.   *Kareem is not sad.*

Numbers:

6- sitta ----------(٦)

7- sabɛa --------(٧)

8- tamanya -----(٨)

9- tesɛa ---------(٩)

10- ɛašara -----(١٠)

Drills

<u>Drill 1:</u> Complete the question word with the appropriate suffix
pronouns (-ak / -ik):

1- izzay- ……. ya Tom ?

2- izzay-…….. ya Dalia ?

3- izzay-…….. ya Sami ?

<u>Drill 2:</u> Use the picture to answer the question:

izzayyak/ik ?

-----------------   ------------------   -----------------

<u>Drill 3:</u> Choose the correct form of adjective:

1- ana ....   (kuwayyis/a)
2- Dalia .... šiwayya .   (zaɛlaan/a)
3- inta .... awi.   (kuwayyis/a)
4- inti ....   (taɛbaan/a)
5- Mary miš ....   (mabsuut/a)
6- Tom miš ...... ana ...... (taɛbaan/a- kuwayyis/a)

<u>Drill 4:</u> Use the picture to answer the question:

1- Mark zaɛlaan ?

2- Linda kuwayyisa ?

3- AHmad mabsuut ?

4- Nadia zaɛlaana ?

33

<u>Drill 5:</u> Fill the blanks with appropriate suffix pronouns (i, ak, ik):

1- inti ɛand… ɛarabiyya ?

2- ya madam Linda ɛand…. awlaad *(children)* ?

3- ana ɛand…. walad wi bint.

4- inta ɛand…. bard ?

5- ana ɛand…. dars ɛarabi *(Arabic lesson)*.

<u>Drill 6:</u> Mention what you have and what you don't:

ɛandi …….. , wi miš ɛandi ……..

<u>Drill 7</u>: Translate into Arabic:

1- I have a car.

2- Do you (m.) have a pen?

3- You (f.) have a house.

4- You (f.) are very well.

5- Are you (m.) sad?

6- I am not sad, but I am tired.

7- I am very sad.

8- You (f.) are not well. You have a cold.

<u>Drill 8</u>: Put the numbers in ascending order:

xamsa – tesɛa – sabɛa – talata – setta – waaHid

<u>Drill 9</u>: Reorder the words and make a sentence:

1- taɛbaana – šiwayya – ana – inta – wi – ?

2- ilHamdu lillah – awi – kuwayyis – ana

3- walla – zaɛlaan – mabsuut – inta – ?

4- ana – ɛandi – miš – wi – bard – kuwayyisa

Listening:

Learn: mašghuula : *busy*
          maɛa   : *with*
          oxti   : *my sister*
          malha   : *what is wrong with her?*

Listen to the dialogue and answer the questions:

1- Circle any word you recognize.
2- Magda is busy with whom?
3- What is wrong with her sister?

Dialogue B:

Magda   : izzayyik ya Maha ! waHaštini !

Maha   : ahlan ahlan ya Magda inti feen !

Magda   : mašghuula šiwayya maɛa Diina oxti.

Maha   : malha Diina ?

Magda   : zaɛlaana šiwayya maɛa goozha.

Maha   : leeh bass kida ?

Magda   : mašaakil ilawlaad zayy ma inti ɛarfa.

Maha   : maɛliš, rabbena maɛaha.

Magda   : šokran ya Maha, ɛayza ašuufik !

Maha   : inša'allah, maɛa issalaama.

Lesson 4

inta mineen ?

Where Are You from?

Lesson Contents:

1- Subject Pronouns (*he, she*)

2- Possessive Pronouns *(his, her)*

3- Nationalities

4- Question Words *(from where?)*

Key Words

huwwa masri
He is Egyptian

hiyya masriyya
She is Egyptian

huwwa amriiki
He is American

hiyya amriikiyya
She is American

huwwa faransi
He is French

hiyya faransiyya
She is French

Masr
ana min Masr
I am from Egypt

Amriika
ana min Amriika
I am from America

Faransa
ana min Faransa
I am from France

DIALOGUE:

inta mineen ? *Where Are You from?*

Mostafa : izzayyak ya Tom ?

Tom : kuwayyis ilHamdu lillah.

Mostafa : inta kanadi ya Tom ?

Tom : la ana miš kanadi, ana amriiki.

Mostafa : wi Linda mineen ?

Tom : hiyya min Faransa.

Mostafa : aah ! hiyya faransiyya miš amriikiyya zayyak !

Tom : la miš amriikiyya, wi inta ya Mostafa mineen ?

Mostafa : ana masri min ilqahira.

Vocabulary

kanadi /-iyya	*Canadian (m., f.)*
amriiki /-iyya	*American (m., f.)*
mineen	*from where (where ...from)*
huwwa / hiyya	*he / she*
min	*from*
Faransa	*France*
faransi /-iyya	*French (m., f.)*
zayyak /-ik	*as / like you (m., f.)*
masri /-iyya	*Egyptian (m., f.)*
ilqahira	*Cairo*

Drill 1: Answer the questions:

1- Tom mineen ?
2- Linda mineen ?
3- Linda zayy Tom ?
4- Mostafa min Amriika ?

Drill 2: Choose the appropriate response:

1- inta mineen ?   a- aywa hiyya masriyya.
2- inti amriikiyya ?   b- la' ana almaniyya.
3- hiyya min Masr ?   c- huwwa min Kanada.
4- Tom mineen ?   d- ana min Faransa.

Drill 3: Right or wrong:

1- Mostafa min Faransa.   (   )
2- Linda amriikiyya.   (   )
3- Tom min Amriika.   (   )
4- Mostafa masri min ilqahira.   (   )
5- Linda faransiyya wi Tom amriiki. (   )

41

Grammar:
Subject Pronouns

In this lesson we'll introduce subject pronouns of 3rd person (singular):

huwwa   *he*

hiyya   *she*

Possessive Pronouns:
Masculine:

* When the word ends with two consonants we insert vowel "**a**" before "**ha**". That change is made to avoid having three consonants in a row.

Subject Pronoun	huwwa	hiyya
Possessive Pronoun	---u	---ha
?alam	?alam**u**	?alam**ha**
ism	ism**u**	isma**ha** *

Feminine:

We learned before that in feminine words we change the feminine suffix "**a**" to "**t**" before we add the possessive pronoun (for pronouns "*ana, inta, inti, huwwa*").

- For Subject Pronoun "**hiyya**", we change that ending "**a**" to "**it**".

** However, when the word ends with two consonants "**šanta**", we change that ending "**a**" to "**it**" for all pronouns.

Subject Pronoun	huwwa	hiyya
Possessive Pronoun	---u	---ha
suura	suurt**u**	suurit**ha** *
šanta	šantit**u** **	šantit**ha** **

Question Word

mineen   *Where ..... from?*

Nationalities

- Names of countries and cities are feminine.
- The process of forming the nationality from the country name:
   a. Drop definition letters "**il**", final long vowel "**a**" or "**ya**" and the feminine ending " **ة a**" from the country name.
   b. add "**i**" for (m.) or "**iyya**" for (f.)

Country:	m.	f.	Pl.
Masr *(Egypt)*	masri	masriyya	masriyyiin
Faransa *(France)*	faransi	faransiyya	faransiyyiin
Amriika *(America)*	amriiki	amriikiyya	amriikiyyiin
Almaania *(Germany)*	almaani	almaaniyya	almaaniyyiin
Kanada *(Canada)*	kanadi	kanadiyya	kanadiyyiin
Itaalia *(Italy)*	itaali	itaaliyya	itaaliyyiin
Issoɛodiyya *(Saudi Arabia)*	soɛodi	soɛodiyya	soɛodiyyiin

Drills

<u>Drill 1</u>: Complete using: **ana, inta, inti, huwwa, hiyya**

1- ismak Saalim, ... soʕodi.

2- ismik Linda, ... amriikiyya.

3- ismaha Suzy, ... faransiyya.

4- ismu Kareem, ... masri.

5- ismi Jack, ... kanadi.

<u>Drill 2</u>: Provide the correct subject pronoun:

1- ------- masriyya ?   - la' an faransiyya.

2- ------- kanadi ya Tom ?   - la' ana amriiki.

3- miin Kareem ?   - --------- zimiili.

4- Mona min Masr.   - ------- masriyya.

5- Linda fi ilbeet ?   - la' ------ miš fi ilbeet.

<u>Drill 3</u>: Reorder the words and make a sentence:

1- ana – amriiki – miš - la'

2- miš – hiyya – zayyak – aah – faransiyya – amriikiyya

3- min – ilqahira – Mostafa – Masr – min

4- mineen – ya – inti – Nadia – ?

<u>Drill 4:</u> Answer the question with "*yes*". Include the nationality
         in your response:

1- Fariid min Masr ?

2- Nabiil min Issoɛodiyya ?

3- Suzy min Faransa ?

4- Tom min Amriika ?

5- Isabel min Itaalia ?

<u>Drill 5:</u> huwwa / hiyya mineen ?
         (Your answer should include both a country and a nationality)

-----------   ----------------   ----------------

-----------   ----------------   ----------------

<u>Drill 6</u>: Choose the appropriate interrogative to complete
each question:

eh, miin, mineen, izzay

1- inti ------- ya Linda ?   - ana min Amriika.

2- -------- di ya Mark ?   - di miraati.

3- -------- da ?   - da kitaab.

4- -------- ya AHmad ?   - kuwayyis

5- ismik --------- ?   - ismi Suzy.

<u>Drill 7</u>: Form questions for these answers:

1- la' ana masri.

2- ismi Tarek.

3- huwwa min Almaania.

4- ana kuwayyisa awi.

5- da zimiili Fariid.

6- di tarabeeza.

7- aywa, ana Diina.

Drill 8: Translate into English:

1- ismi Kareem, ana masri.

2- ismu AHmad, huwwa soʕodi.

3- irraagil da faransi wi issitt di asbaaniyya.

4- da walad amriiki, huwwa ismu Jack.

5- inti kanadiyya ?

6- hiyya ismaha Sofia, hiyya itaaliyya.

Drill 9: Translate into Arabic:

1- He is from Italy.

2- Where are you (f.) from?

3- She is Egyptian.

4- I am French.

5- You (m.) are from Saudi Arabia.

6- Mona is from Cairo, Egypt.

Listening:

Learn: raayiH : *going (m.)*
  isseef : *summer*
  ɛaayiš : *living (m.)*

Listen to the dialogue and answer the questions:

1- Circle any word you recognize.
2- Where is Tarek going this summer?
3- Is Tom American or French?

Dialogue B:

Samiira : raayiH feen ya Tarek isseef da ?

Tarek : raayiH li Tom fi Faransa !

Samiira : Tom saHbak ?

Tarek : aywa.

Samiira : huwwa miš Tom amriiki ?

Tarek : aywa, bass ɛaayiš fi Faransa.

Samiira : aah ɛašaan kida !

Tarek : wi inti rayHa feen issana di ?

Samiira : miš rayHa, ?aɛda fi Masr.

Tarek : tayyib, ɛayza Haaga min Faransa ?

Samiira : la' šokran, aggaaza saɛiida inša'allah !

Lesson 5

saakin feen ?

Where Do You Live?

Lesson Contents:

1- Subject Pronouns (more) (*you {m., f.}*)

2- Subject Pronouns *(pl.) (we, you{pl.}, they)*

3- Active participle *(living)*

4- Adverb *(beside, in front of)*

5- Question Words *(where?)*

6- Numbers 11-20

Key Words

saakin feen ? *Where do you live?*

šaariε eh ? *What street?*

nimra kaam ? *What number?*

Key Words

iHna   *we*

intu   *you (pl.)*

homma   *they*

gamb *beside* - ʔoddaam *in front of*

-- ilʕarabiyya gamb iššagara ʔoddaam ilbeet
The car is beside the tree, in front of the house.

51

DIALOGUE:

saakin feen ? *Where Do You Live?*

Sami : Hadritak saakin feen ya ostaaz Fariid ?

Fariid : ana saakin fi ilmaɛaadi.

Sami : šaariɛ eh ?

Fariid : šaariɛ tesɛa.

Sami : feen fi šaariɛ tesɛa ?

Fariid : gamb matɛam Kentucky.

Sami : nimra kaam ?

Fariid : nimra itnašar.

Vocabulary

Hadritak/-ik	*you (m., f. {for respect})*
saakin /sakna/-iin	*living (m., f., pl.)*
feen	*where?*
fi	*in*
šaariɛ	*street*
tesɛa	*nine*
gamb	*beside*
matɛam	*restaurant*
nimra	*number*
kaam	*how many?/how much?(what number)*
itnašar	*twelve*

<u>Drill 1:</u> Answer the questions:

1- Fariid saakin feen ?

2- huwwa saakin fi šaariɛ eh ?

3- gamb eh ?

4- nimra kaam ?

<u>Drill 2:</u> Choose the appropriate response:

1- nimra kaam ?

a- šaariɛ Mostafa Kaamil.

2- inti sakna feen ?

b- talata.

3- šaariɛ eh ?

c- ana saakin fi izzamaalik.

4- Hadritak saakin feen ?

d- gamb bank CIB.

5- gamb eh ?

e- ana sakna fi ilmaɛaadi.

<u>Drill 3:</u> Right or wrong:

1- Fariid saakin gamb Kentucky.   (   )

2- Fariid saakin fi izzamaalik.   (   )

3- Fariid saakin fi šaariɛ tesɛa.   (   )

4- matɛam Kentucky fi šaariɛ xamsa.   (   )

Grammar:

Pronouns:

These are the plural forms of the subject pronouns of 1st, 2nd and 3rd person:

iHna   *we*

intu   *you (pl.)*

homma   *they*

Active Participles:

An active participle is an adjective derived from a verb and have a meaning closely associated with that of the verb. It is performing the action indicated by the verb.

Masculine:
ana/ inta/ huwwa   saakin   *(living)*

Feminine:
ana/ inti/ hiyya   sakna

Plural:
iHna/ intu/ homma   sakniin

Adverbs:

gamb	*beside, next to*
?udaam	*in front of, across from*

Question Words:

feen	*Where?*
kaam	*How many?/ How much?*

Notes:

There is a formal way to address people who are not known to the speaker or who need to be respect.

Hadritak	*you (m.) /respect*
Hadritik	*you (f.) /respect*

Numbers:

11- Hidaašar -------(١١)

12- itnaašar -------(١٢)

13- talataašar ------(١٣)

14- arbaεtašar -----(١٤)

15- xamastašar ----(١٥)

16- sittašar ---------(١٦)

17- sabaεtašar -----(١٧)

18- tamantašar -----(١٨)

19- tesaεtašar ------(١٩)

20- εišriin ---------(٢٠)

Drills

Drill 1 : Provide these sentences with the appropriate subject pronoun:

ana, inta, inti, huwwa, hiyya, iHna, intu, homma

1- .... sakniin fi ilmaɛaadi.   (Diina wi Suzy)

2- .... sakna feen ?

3- ya Mark wi ya Mona, ... sakniin fi izzamaalik ?

4- .... saakin gamb issifaara.

5- .... faransiyyiin.   (ana wi goozi)

6- ya Linda, ... sakna fi šaariɛ eh ?

Drill 2: Provide the appropriate subject pronoun:

1- ------- mineen ?   - iHna min Amriika.

2- Mark wi Linda mineen ?   - ------- min Kanada.

3- intu sakniin feen ?   - ----- sakniin fi ilmaɛaadi.

4- ana wi Tom min Amriika.   - aah, ----- amriikiyiin !!

5- inta masri ?   - la', ------ sodaani.

6- Mona sakna feen ?   - ----- sakna fi izzamaalik.

<u>Drill 3:</u> Use the appropriate active participle:

saakin, sakna, sakniin:

1- intu……… gamb issifaara ?

2- iHna ………. fi ilmaɛaadi .

3- Hasan wi Layla ………. fi izzamaalik.

4- inta ………. gamb Jack ?

5- inti ………. feen ?

6- ana ……… ?oddaam ilmadrasa *(school)* ilamriikiyya.

<u>Drill 4:</u> Choose the appropriate interrogative to complete:

eh, kaam, feen, mineen

1- intu sakniin ------- ?   - sakniin fi ilmaɛaadi.

2- beetak nimra ------ ?   - nimra talata.

3- il?alam --------?   - ɛala ittarabeeza.

4- homma -------- ?   - min Faransa.

5- sakna fi šaariɛ ----- ?   - fi šaariɛ tessɛa .

58

<u>Drill 5</u>: Translate into Arabic:

1- I live beside my colleague Nadia.

2- They live in front of the American school.

3- Do you (m.) live on street 11?

4- He lives beside a bank.

5- We live in Zamaalik near the Pizza Hut restaurant.

6- She lives on street 20 and in number 13.

<u>Drill 6</u> : Complete the following sentences using the numbers
                     in Arabic:

1-iHna sakniin fi šaariɛ ……...   (15)

2- AHmad saakin fi beet nimra ……..   (8)

3- ana sakna fi šaariɛ …… maɛa šaariɛ …..   (17, 20)

4- intu sakniin fi šaariɛ ….. nimra ……   (9,3)

<u>Drill 7</u>: Translate into English:

- sittašar   - Hidašar

- itnašar   - tesaɛtašar

- ɛišriin   - sabaɛtašar

<u>Drill 8</u>: Reorder the words and make a sentence:

1- saakin – ilmaɛaadi – ana – fi
2- gamb – tesɛa – šaariɛ – Mostafa Kaamil – šaariɛ
3- feen – sakniin – intu - ?
4- sakna – Linda – matɛam – Pizza Hutt – gamb
5- ilmadrasa - Fariid - ?oddaam - saakin - ilamriikiyya

<u>Drill 9</u>: Translate the following dialogue:

Sami   : nimrit teliifoonak kaam ya Mostafa ?

Mostafa : itneen sabɛa tisɛa talaata sitta itneen sitta
            tamanya.

Sami   : marra tanya min fadlak.

Listening:

Learn: rayHa   : *going*
                       Hafla   : *party*
                       nafs ilmakaan : *same place*
                       fihimt   : *I understood*

Listen to the dialogue and answer the questions:

1- Circle any word you recognize.
2- Where is Nora going?
3- Where does Nadia live?

Dialogue B:

Kaamil : eh iššiyaaka di ya Nora !

Nora   : asli rayHa Hafla innaharda ɛand Nadia saHbiti.

Kaamil : wallahi ! sakna feen saHbitik ?

Nora   : fi iddo??i, gamb pizza hut.

Kaamil : gamb pizza hut ! šaariɛ eh ?

Nora   : šaariɛ Qambiiz.

Kaamil : miš maɛ?uul, nimra kaam ?

Nora   : nimra talata, fiih eh ?

Kaamil : asl ana kamaan raayiH Hafla fi nafs ilmakaan.

Nora   : ɛand miin ?

Kaamil : ɛand maHmoud saHbi.

Nora   : aah fihimt , asl gooz Nadia ismu maHmoud .

Lesson 6

fi ikkafitiria !

At the Coffee Shop !

Lesson Contents:

1- Adjectives *(hot, cold)*

2- Active participle *(wanting)*

3- Question Words and their negative forms *(is there?, are there?, there is no)*

Key Words

šaay *tea*

ʔahwa *coffee*

ʕasiir farawla
strawberry juice

ʕasiir bortoʔaan
orange juice

ʕasiir lamon
lemon juice

mayya
water

Haaga saʔʕa
soft drinks

63

Key Words

ʕeeš *bread* beed *egg* gibna *cheese* merabba *jam*

salata *salad* šorba *soup* rozz *rice* makaroona *pasta*

firaax *chicken* samak *fish* laHma *meat* kabaab *shish kebab*

DIALOGUE:

fi ikkafitiria !   *At the Coffee Shop!:*

Mark   : ya metr!

ilmetr   : aywa, ayy xidma ?

Mark   : ɛaayiz šaay minfadlalk !

Linda   : ɛandak Haaga sa?ɛ a ?

ilmetr   : fiih bibsi wi ɛasiir.

Linda   : ɛayza ɛasiir borto?aan.

ilmetr   : Haadir, ayy xidma tanya ?

Mark   : la, šokran. ilHisaab minfadlak !

Linda   : minfadlak, ilHammaam feen ?

Vocabulary

ayy xidma ?	*Can I help you?*
ɛaayiz /ɛayza/-iin	*wanting (m., f., pl.)*
šaay	*tea*
Haaga sa?ɛ a	*soft drink*
fiih	*there is, there are*
ɛasiir	*juice*
borto?aan	*orange*
Haadir	*Ok*
ayy xidma tanya ?	*any other service?*
šokran	*thanks*
ilHisaab	*the bill*
minfadlak/-ik	*please (m., f.)*
ilHammaam	*the bathroom*

Drill 1: Answer the questions:

1- Mark ɛaayiz eh ?

2- miin maɛa Mark ?

3- homma feen ?

4- miin ɛaayiz ɛasiir ?

Drill 2: Choose the appropriate response:

1- fiih ɛasiir ?   a- la šokran.

2- ayy xidma tanya ?   b- Haadir.

3- ɛaayiz šaay minfadlak.   c- aywa ayy xidma ?

4- ya metr !   d- aywa ɛayza ɛasiir eh ?

Drill 2: Right or wrong:

1- Linda ɛayza ɛasiir farawla.   (   )

2- Mark ɛaayiz ?ahwa.   (   )

3- Mark ɛaayiz šaay.   (   )

4- hiyya ɛayza Haaga sa?ɛ a.   (   )

Grammar:

Adjectives:

In Arabic, the adjectives follow the nouns they modify. So you say "*a tea hot*" instead of "*a hot tea*". Adjectives have to agree in gender with the nouns that they modify.

Masculine	Feminine	
------	-----**a**	
saaʔiɛ	saʔɛ **a**	*cold*
soxn	soxn**a**	*hot*

Example:

šaay soxn
hot tea

Haaga saʔɛ a
something cold

Question Word:

fiih   *Is there? / Are there?*

Negative Form:

mafiiš   *There isn't / There aren't*

Active Participles:

Masculine:
ana/ inta/ huwwa   ɛaayiz   *(wanting)*

Feminine:
ana/ inti/ hiyya   ɛayza

Plural:
iHna/ intu/ homma   ɛayziin

Notes

1- minfadlak /ik/uku: *please (m./ f./ pl.)*

It is used to request a favour or an action from someone else. It has three forms (m., f., pl.), depending on who is being addressed.

2- Haadir:

It has a meaning of "*ok*" as a response to a request or order

-ɛaayiz fingaan ?ahwa minfadlak !

--Haadir

Drills

Drill 1 : Put the adjectives in the right gender:

1- ilʔahwa miš ----- ɛaayiz ʔahwa tanya.   (soxn)

2- ɛaayiz ayy ɛasiir ------, fiih eh ?   (saaʔiɛ)

3- ɛayziin Haaga -----, walla ----- ?   (soxn, saaʔiɛ)

4- mafiiš mayya ----- .   (soxn)

5- ilmayya ----- miš -----.   (saaʔiɛ, soxn)

6- feen Samiir   ?   huwwa -----   ?   (taɛbaan)

Drill 2: Fill the blanks with **minfadlak** or **minfadlik**:

1- ------- ya Dalia, ɛayza mayya.

2- ya Mark, ɛaayiz ʔalam ---------.

3- ya metr, ɛaayiz ɛasiir farawla ---------.

4- ya madam Linda, nimrit tilifonik kaam --------- ?

5- ya aanesa, feen šaariɛ tessɛa -------- ?

6- -------- ya ostaaz AHmad, fiih tilifoon hina ?

7- ismik eh -------- ?

<u>Drill 3</u>: Provide the following sentences with the appropriate form
of Ɛaayiz, Ɛayza , Ɛayziin:

1- ana ---------- fingaan šaay minfadlak.

2- iHna ----------- mayya.

3- inta --------- miin ?

4- homma ----------- ?ahwa.

5- hiyya ---------- eh ?

6- inti --------- ilmodiir *(the director)* ?

<u>Drill 4</u>: Answer the questions:

<u>Example</u>:   fiih Ɛasiir borto?aan ?

            - aywa fiih Ɛasiir borto?aan.

            - la' mafiiš Ɛasiir borto?aan.

1- fiih matƐam ?odaam ilbeet ?

2- fiih fingaan ?ahwa Ɛala ittarabeeza ?

3- fiih mayya sa?Ɛ a ?

4- fiih Ɛarabiyya fi iššaariƐ ?

5- fiih ?alam gamb ikkitaab ?

6- fiih raagil fi ilmaktab ?

7- fiih sitt amrikiyya hina ?

<u>Drill 5:</u> Make your order for each meal:

ya metr , --

1- fitaar *breakfast*

2– ghada *lunch*

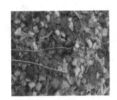  

3– ɛaša *dinner*

Drill 6: Reorder the words and make a sentence:

1- ع asiir – minfadlak – ana – ع aayiz – borto?aan

2- xidma – ya – tanya – madam – ayy – ?

3- soxna – walla – ع ayza – sa?ع a – Haaga - ?

4- šaay – Mark – soxn – ع aayiz

5- ع ayza – wi – šorba – ana – samak

Drill 7: Translate into Arabic:

1- He wants rice and chicken.

2- Can I help you?

3- They want coffee and mango juice.

4- Do you want something hot or cold?

5- We want salad and meat.

6- I want a cup of tea and water.

7- The bill, please.

Listening:

Learn: tišrabi   : *you(f.) drink*
                          ɛala fikra : *by the way*
                          il'akl   : *the food*
                          aaxud   : *I take*

Listen to the dialogue and answer the questions:

1- Circle any word you recognize.
2- What will Nora drink?
3- What kind of food do they have?

Dialogue B:

Nora   : ilHafla gamiila awi ya Nadia !

Nadia : mercy ya Nora, tišrabi eh ya Habibti ?

Nora   : ayy Haaga saʔɛ a.

Nadia : wi inta ya ostaaz Kaamil ?

Kaamil : la' šokran kamaan šiwayya.

Nadia   : ɛala fikra fiih sandawitšaat firaax wi kofta
             wi Hagaat kitiira, itfaddalu !

Nora   : tayyib taɛala ya Kaamil niruuH nišuuf.
            il'akl kitiir wi ana miš ɛarfa aaxud eh.

Kaamil : ana Haxud salata wi sandawitš firaax.

Nora   : wi ana kamaan Haxud zayyak !

Lesson 7

innaharda yoom eh ?

What Day Is Today?

Lesson Contents:

1- Days of the week and months

2- Adverbs

3- Telling Time

4- Question Word *(why?)*

5- Object Pronouns *(see you {m., f.})*

Key Words

issaaعa kaam ?
What time is it?

issaaعa xamsa.
It is five o'clock.

innaharda yoom eh ?   *What day is today?*

issaaɛa kaam ?

issaaɛa itneen

issaaɛa itneen wi xamsa

issaaɛa itneen illa xamsa

issaaɛa itneen wi ɛašara

issaaɛa itneen illa ɛašara

issaaɛa itneen wi robɛ

issaaɛa itneen illa robɛ

issaaɛa itneen wi tilt

issaaɛa itneen illa tilt

issaaɛa itneen wi noss
illa xamsa

issaaɛa itneen wi noss

issaaɛa itneen wi noss
wi xamsa

ayaam ilisbuuɛ
days of the week

šuhuur issana
months of the year

issabt	*Saturday*	yanaayir	*January*
ilHadd	*Sunday*	febraayir	*February*
ilitneen	*Monday*	maaris	*March*
ittalaat	*Tuesday*	ibriil	*April*
ilarbaɛ	*Wednesday*	maayu	*May*
ilxamiis	*Thursday*	yonyu	*June*
iggomɛa	*Friday*	yolyu	*July*
		aghostos	*August*
		sebtamber	*September*
		oktobar	*October*
		nofamber	*November*
		desamber	*December*

DIALOGUE:

innaharda yoom eh ?   *What Day Is Today?*:

Diina   : ya Mona, innaharda yoom eh ?

Mona   : innaharda ilitneen, leeh ?

Diina   : fiih igtimaaε yoom ittalaat.

Mona   : issaaεa kaam ?

Diina   : issaaεa tamanya.

Mona   : issobH walla billeel ?

Diina   : issobH.

Mona   : tayyib, ašuufik bokra inša' allah !

Vocabulary

innaharda	*today*
yoom	*day*
ilitneen	*Monday*
leeh	*why*
igtimaaε	*meeting*
ittalaat	*Tuesday*
issaaεa kaam ?	*What time is it?*
issobH	*in the morning*
billeel	*in the evening*
ašuufak/-ik	*I will see you (m., f.)*
bokra	*tomorrow*
inša' allah	*If God wills*

Drill 1: Answer the questions:

1- iligtimaaε yoom eh ?

2- iligtimaaε issaaεa kaam ?

3- innaharda yoom eh ?

4- iligtimaaε issobH walla billeel ?

Drill 2: Choose the appropriate response:

1- issaaεa kaam ?   a- billeel.

2- innaharda yoom eh ?   b- tamanya.

3- issobH walla billeel ?   c- inša' allah.

4- ašuufak bokra.   d- ilitneen.

Drill 2: Right or wrong:

1- iligtimaaε bokra.   (   )

2- innaharda yoom ilitneen.   (   )

3- iligtimaaε billeel.   (   )

4- iligtimaaε issaaεa tamanya.   (   )

Grammar:

Adverb

issobH   *in the morning*

iddohr   *at noon*

baɛd iddohr   *in the afternoon*

billeel   *in the evening*

Object Pronouns:

Subject Pronoun	inta	inti
Object Pronoun	---ak	---ik
ašuuf *(I see)*	ašuuf**ak**	ašuuf**ik**

Question Word

leeh   *Why?*

Notes

"**walla**" is used when choosing between two things in a question.

walla   *or*

Drills

Drill 1: issaaʕa kaam ?   *What time is it?*:

- 2:20
- 1:45
- 7:35
- 8:25
- 3:15

- 10:10
- 5:05
- 12:30
- 11:40
- 4:50

Drill 2: issaaʕa kaam ?   *What time is it?*:

....

....

Drill 3: What time is ....?:

1- ilHafla *(the party)* issaaɛa kaam ?

2- iligtimaaɛ issaaɛa kaam ?

3- dars ilɛarabi issaaɛa kaam ?

4- ilfilm issaaɛa kaam ?

5- ilaxbaar *(the news)* issaaɛa kaam ?

6- ilɛaša issaaɛa kaam ?

Drill 4: What day is ....?:

1- innaharda yoom eh ?

2- bokra yoom eh ?

3- imbaariH *(yesterday)* yoom eh ?

4- baɛd bokra *(the day after tomorrow)* yoom eh ?

5- ilagaaza *(the holiday)* imta *(when)* ?

6- ilHafla imta ?

7- iligtimaaɛ imta ?

Drill 5: What month is ....?:

1- iHna fi šahr eh ?

2- ɛiid miiladak/ik *(your birthday)* fi šahr eh ?

3- Ramadan fi šahr eh ?

4- agaaztak/ik *(your vacation)* fi šahr eh ?

5- ikkerismas fi šahr eh ?

Drill 6: Complete each sentence with the correct day:

1- innaharda ittalaat wi bokra ....

2- imbaariH ilxamiis wi innaharda ....

3- bokra issabt wi baɛd bokra ....

4- imbaariH ilarbaɛ wi awwil imbaariH *(the day before yesterday)* ......

5- imbaariH .... wi innaharda iggomɛa

Drill 7: Translate into Arabic:

1- Today is Sunday.

2- What time is the meeting?

3- Yesterday was a holiday.

4- The party is on Thursday at 7:00.

5- See you (m.) tomorrow morning.

6- See you (f.) at the party on Friday.

7- The meeting is the day after tomorrow.

Listening:

Learn: mawaɛiid : *appointments*
        ilwizaara : *the ministry*
        hidiyya : *gift*
        nisiit : *I forgot*

Listen to the dialogue and answer the questions:

1- Circle any word you recognize.
2- What is he going to do today?
3- When is his wife's birthday?

Dialogue B:

ilmodiir : ɛandi mawaɛiid eh innaharda ?

issikirtiira : innaharda issaaɛa waHda fiih igtimaaɛ fi
ilwizaara .wi issaaɛa talata wi noss fiih ghada
fi simiramiis wi billeel fiih Hafla ɛašaan ɛiid
milaad ilmadaam.

ilmodiir : leeh innaharda kaam ?

issikirtiira : innaharda xamsa yonyo.

ilmodiir : yaah ! da ana nisiit xaalis.

issikirtiira : ana gibt ittorta wi ilhidiyya wi baɛat ward
kamaan.

issikirtiira : ya salaam ya Diina, inti sikirtiira hayla.

Lesson 8

iššanta feen ?

Where Is the Bag?

Lesson Contents:

1- Prepositions

2- The Definite Article *(the)*

Key Words

ilfingaan ع<u>ala</u> ittarabeeza.

The cup is on the table.

iššanta <u>taHt</u> ittarabeeza.

The bag is under the table.

issuura <u>foo?</u> ittarabeeza.

The picture is above the table.

DIALOGUE:

iššanta feen ? *Where Is the Bag?:*

Fariid   : ya Kareem iššanta feen ?

Kareem : ɛala ittarabeeza.

Fariid   : mafiiš Haaga ɛala ittarabeeza.

Kareem : tayyib šuuf taHt ikkursi.

Fariid   : mafiiš bardu.

Kareem : yimkin foo? ittilifizyoon !

Fariid   : aywa hina, šokran ya Kareem.

Kareem : ɛafwan.

Vocabulary

ɛala	*on*
mafiiš Haaga	*nothing (lit.: there is not anything)*
tayyib	*OK*
šuuf/i	*look (m., f.)*
taHt	*under*
kursi	*chair*
bardu	*also*
yimkin	*maybe*
foo?	*above, over*
tilifizyoon	*T.V.*
hina	*here*
ɛafwan (ilɛafwu)	*You are welcome*

Drill 1: Answer the questions:

1- Fariid ɛaayiz eh ?

2- iššanta ɛala ittarabeeza ?

3- fiih šanta taHt ikkursi ?

4- fiih eh foo? ittilifizyoon ?

Drill 2: Choose the appropriate response:

1- šuuf taHt ilmaktab.   a- ɛafwan !

2- iššanta feen ?   b- mafiiš.

3- šokran !   c- ɛala ittarabeeza.

Drill 3: Right or wrong:

1- iššanta ɛala ittarabeeza.   (   )

2- Kareem ɛaayiz iššanta.   (   )

3- issaaɛa foo? ittilifizyoon.   (   )

4- mafiiš šanta taHt ikkursi.   (   )

5- ittilifizyoon taHt iššanta .   (   )

Grammar:

The Definite Article

The definite article (*the*) is "**il**" and is joined to the noun.

il   *the*

- The "**l**" is pronounced if the noun begins with a moon letter.

Moon Letters: $a - b - H - x - \varepsilon - gh - f - ? - m - h - w - y$

<u>il</u>baab   *the door*

- if the noun begins with a sun letter the "**l**" disappears and the first consonant is doubled:

Sun Letters: $t - g - d - r - z - s - š - k - l - n$

<u>it</u>tarabeeza   *the table*

Prepositions

fi	*in*
εala	*on*
taHt	*under*
gamb	*beside/ next to/ near*
foo?	*over/ above*
been	*in between*
wara	*behind*
?oddaam	*in front of*

Drills

Drill 1: Make these words definite:

1- kitaab.	6- sitt	11- kobbaaya
2- tarabeeza	7- fingaan	12- ɛarabiyya
3- baab	8- walad	13- bint
4- raagil	9- zimiil	14- beet
5- saaɛa	10- šaariɛ	15- šanta

Drill 2: Complete the sentences with a preposition:

gamb, taHt, wara, ɛala, foo?, ?oddaam

1- ikkitaab ……… il?alam.

2- ilbeet ……….. ilmatɛam.

3- iššanta ……… ittarabeeza.

4- ikkitaab ……… iššanta.

5- ilbaab …….. irraagil.

6- ilfingaan ……….. ittilifizyoon.

<u>Drill 3:</u> Describe each picture:

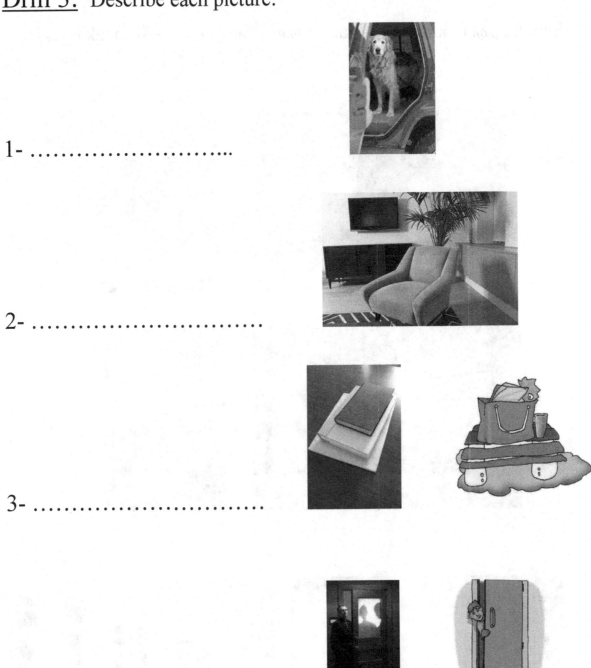

1- ……………………...

2- …………………………

3- …………………………

4- ………………………………

Drill 4: Describe the picture:

kanaba *(sofa)* - kalb *(dog)* - zarʕ *(plant)* - faaza *(vase)* - šibbaak *(window)*

Drill 5: Translate into Arabic:

1- Look (f.) under the table.

2- The chair is in front of the door.

3- There is nothing beside the house.

4- The man is in front of the office.

5- The girl is beside the boy.

6- The picture is above the table.

7- Look (m.) over the desk.

8- The bag is under the chair.

Listening:

Learn: naddafi : *you (f.) clean*
        aHutt : *I put*
        abajora : *lamp*

Listen to the dialogue and answer the questions:

1- Circle any word you recognize.
2- Where will Fatma put the vase?
3- Where is the picture?

Dialogue B:

ilmadaam   : ya Fatma, naddafi taHt ikkanaba.

iššaghghaala : Haadir ya madam, aHutt ilfaaza di feen ?

ilmadaam   : Hutti ilfaaza ɛala ittarabeeza.

iššaghghaala : tayyib wi ilabajora ?

ilmadaam   : Huttiha hina gamb ilfaaza wi haati izzarɛ
               illi wara ikkursi wi Huttih been ikkursi wi
               ikkanaba.

iššaghghaala : Haadir, Haaga tanya ya madam ?

ilmadaam   : aywa naddafi issora illi foo? ittilifizyoon.

iššaghghaala : Haadir ya madam.

Lesson 9

raayiH feen ?

Where Are You Going?

Lesson Contents:

1- Active Participles *(going)*

2- Noun-Adjective Phrases and Sentences

3- Adjectives

4- Colors

Key Words

west ilbalad _downtown_

sifaara _embassy_

fondo? _hotel_

Adjectives:

kibiir/a *big* & soghayyar/a *small*

tawiil/a *tall* & ?osayyar/a *short*

gidiid/a *new*   ?adiim/a *old*

gamiil/a *beautiful*   wiHiš/wiHša *bad- ugly*

ghaali/a *expensive*   rixiis/a *cheap*

Colors:

aHmar / Hamra   *red*

asfar / safra   *yellow*

axdar / xadra   *green*

azra? / zar?a   *blue*

abyad / beeda   *white*

iswid / sooda   *black*

DIALOGUE:

raayiH feen ? *Where Are You Going?*

Mona   : ya Ahmad raayiH feen ?

AHmad : raayiH issifaara ilamriikiyya.

Mona   : ana kamaan rayHa west ilbalad.

AHmad : rayHa feen fi west ilbalad.

Mona   : rayHa fondo? helton, ɛayza gazma sooda
          gidiida ɛašaan ilHafla.

AHmad : tayyib, yalla biina.

Vocabulary

raayiH /rayHa /-iin	*going (m., f., pl.)*
issifaara	*embassy*
ilamriikiyya	*American*
kamaan	*also*
west ilbalad	*downtown*
fondo?	*hotel*
gazma	*shoes*
iswid/soda	*black (m., f.)*
gidiid/a	*new (m., f.)*
tayyib	*OK!*
yalla biina	*let us go*

<u>Drill 1</u>: Answer the questions:

1- AHmad raayiH feen ?

2- issifaara ilamriikiyya feen ?

3- Mona rayHa feen ?

4- hiyya ɛayza eh ?   leeh ?

<u>Drill 2</u>: Choose the appropriate response:

1- inti rayHa west ilbalad ?   a- la hiyya rayHa ilfondo?.

2- Mona rayHa issifaara ?   b- raayiH ilmatɛam issiini.

3- raayiH feen ?   c- aywa yalla biina.

<u>Drill 3</u>: Right or wrong:

1- Mona rayHa ilfondo?.   (   )

2- AHmad raayiH issifaara ilfaransiyya.   (   )

3- AHmad wi Mona rayHiin west ilbalad.   (   )

4- hiyya rayHa ilmaɛaadi.   (   )

5- huwwa raayiH fondo? helton.   (   )

Grammar:

Noun-Adjective Phrases and Sentences:

Adjectives have two functions:

    a. As modifiers, they agree with nouns in definiteness and indefiniteness:

sifaara amriikiyya	*indefinite. phrase: (an American embassy)*
issifaara ilamriikiyya	*def. phrase: (the American embassy)*
matɛam ghaaly	*indefinite phrase: (an expensive restaurant)*
ilmatɛam ilghaaly	*def. phrase: (the expensive restaurant)*

    b- As predicates, they don't agree with nouns in definiteness:

issifaara amriikiyya	*Sentence: (The embassy is American.)*
ilmatɛam ghaaly	*Sentence: (The restaurant is expensive)*

101

Active Participles

Masculine:

ana/ inta/ huwwa   raayiH   *(going)*

Feminine:

ana/ inti/ hiyya   rayHa

Plural:

iHna/ intu/ homma   rayHiin

Drills

<u>Drill 1:</u> What is that? (Give one color for each.)

<u>Drill 2</u>: Complete:

1- iggazma di miš gidiida, hiyya ....

2- issit di miš wiHša, hiyya ....

3- ilɛarabiyya di miš rixiisa, hiyya ....

<u>Drill 3</u>: Use the appropriate active participle:
raayiH, rayHa, rayHiin:

1- inta .... feen ?

2- hiyya miš.......... issifaara bokra.

3- Hasan .... ilbeet.

4- iHna .... west ilbalad.

5- inti .... ilfondo? imta ?

6- miin .... issifaara ?

7- homma .... **šarm iššeex** bokra.

<u>Drill 4</u>: Translate into Arabic:

1- The pen is green.

2- The new pen is green.

3- I want a big cup.

4- This is an expensive book.

5- Where is the blue bag?

6- I would like a white cheese.

7- Are you going to the new restaurant?

8- He is in the black car.

9- We are living in the white house.

10-This is a bad picture.

<u>Drill 5:</u> Translate into English:

1- ?alam rixiis

2- ilfingaan ilazra?

3- sitt tawiila

4- issifaara ilmasriyya

5- ikkitaab gidiid

6- ilmaktab ikkibiir

7- ilbeet axdar

8- ilbint taɛbaana

9- ittarabeeza il?adiima

10- issuura gamiila

11- iššaay issoxn

12- ilɛasiir saa?iɛ

13- ɛarabiyya safra

14- iššanta ilbeeda

15- saaɛa soghayyara

16- kursi iswid

<u>Drill 6:</u> Reorder the words and make a sentence:

1- kamaan – west – ana – rayyiH – ilbalad

2- feen – ya– Sonya – rayHa – madam –   ?

3- rayHiin – tayyib – intu – biina – ilmatɛam – yalla

4- issifaara – walla – hiyya – ilfondo? – rayHa – ?

Listening:

Learn: ma?aas   : *size*
                     sabɛa wi talatiin : *thirty-seven*
                     bikaam   : *What is the price?*

Listen to the dialogue and answer the questions:

1- Circle any word you recognize.
2- What does she want to buy?
3- What is the size of the shoes?

Dialogue B:

Mona : ɛayza iggazma di minfadlik !

ilbayyaaɛa : anhi gazma ya madam ?

Mona : issooda illi gamb iššanta ikkibiira di.

ilbayyaaɛa : ma?aas kaam ?

Mona : sabɛa wi talatiin.

ilbayyaaɛa : tayyib, tiHibbi tišuufi iššanta kamaan ?

Mona : la', ɛayza ašuuf iššanta issoghayyara !

ilbayyaaɛa : Haadir itfaddali ya madam.

Mona : iggazma kuwayyisa, wi iššanta kamaan gamiila, bikaam iggazma wi iššanta ?

ilbayyaaɛa : iggazma bi miyya wi xamsiin gineh wi iššanta bi miteen wi talatiin.

Mona : itfaddali ilfiluus !

ilbayyaaɛa : šukran ya madam, alf mabruuk.

Lesson 10

ɛaayiz taksi

Taking a Taxi

Lesson Contents:

1- Imperative (Giving Directions)
   (Go straight ahead, right, left)
2- Ordinal Numbers

Key Words

ʕalatuul   *straight ahead*

šimaal   yimiin

left   *right*

DIALOGUE:

ɛaayiz taksi ! *Taking a Taxi!*

AHmad   : taksi!

issawwaa? : aywa, raayiH feen ?

AHmad   : west ilbalad .

issawwaa? : itfaddal.

baɛd šiwayya

issawwaa? : feen bizzabt ?

AHmad   : imši ɛalatuul, xušš yimiin iššaariɛ iggay,
            aywa hina kuwayyis, itfaddal ilfiluus.

issawwaa? : šokran, maɛa issalaama.

Vocabulary

sawwaa?	*driver*
itfaddal/i/u	*get in (m., f., pl.)*
baɛd šiwayya	*after awhile*
bizzabt	*exactly*
imši/i/u	*go/ walk (m., f., pl.)*
ɛalatuul	*straight ahead*
xušš/i/u	*enter (m., f., pl.)*
yimiin	*right*
iššaariɛ iggay	*the coming street*
ilfiluus	*money*

<u>Drill 1:</u> Choose the appropriate response:

1- taksi !   a- šokran !

2- raayiH feen ?   b- raayiH west ilbalad.

3- feen bizzabt ?   c- aywa, itfaddal.

4- itfaddal ilfiluus.   d- xušš awwil šaariε yimiin .

<u>Drill 2:</u> Right or wrong:

1- Ahmad raayiH ilfondo?.   (   )

2- Mona fi ittaksi.   (   )

3- AHmad raayiH west ilbalad.   (   )

<u>Drill 3:</u> Reorder the words and make a sentence:

1- yimiin – imši – baεdeen – wi – εalatuul – xušš

2- ilfiluus – kuwayyis – itfaddal – hina

3- bizzabt – feen – raayiH – ?

Grammar:

Imperative (Giving Directions):

m.	f.	pl,
--------	------i	------u
imši	imšii	imšu	(go)
xušš	xušši	xuššu	(enter/turn)

Ordinal Numbers:

awwil	*first*	saatit- saadis	*sixth*
taani	*second*	saabiɛ	*seventh*
taalit	*third*	taamin	*eighth*
raabiɛ	*fourth*	taasiɛ	*ninth*
xaamis	*fifth*	ɛaašir	*tenth*

** awwil šaariɛ xušš yimiin   *(First street turn right)*

Notes:

The word "**itfaddal**" is used for offering a favor or action to someone else (come in, here you are, offering someone food etc.).

It has three forms *(m., f., pl.)*, depending on who is being addressed.

itfaddal   *(m.)*

itfaddali   *(f.)*

itfaddalu   *(pl.)*

Drills

Drill 1: Fill the blanks with an appropriate verb in its correct form:

imši – xušš

1- min fadlak ……… yimiin.

2- ya madaam……… awwil šaariɛ yimiin.

3- ya Hasan ……… ɛalatuul wi baɛdeen …… šimaal.

4- itfaddalu ……… ilmaktab da.

5- Hadritik, …… ɛalatuul , wi taani šaari ɛ…….yimiin.

Drill 2: Translate into English:

1- raayiH feen bizzabt ?

2- imši ɛalatuul wi taalit šaariɛ yimiin.

3- hiyya rayHa šaariɛ ɛišriin.

4- awwil šaariɛ xušš yimiin wi baɛdeen xušš šimaal.

5- ana saakin fi xaamis beet ɛala ilyimiin.

6- iHna sakniin fi awwil beet fi iššaariɛ da.

7- xušš taani šaariɛ yimiin wi baɛdeen imši ɛalatuul.

<u>Drill 3</u>: Make questions and answers, as in the example:

Ex: - maHatit il?atr *(the train station)* feen ?   (4)

--imši ɛalatuul, wi xušš awwil šaariɛ yimiin,
    maHatit il?atr ɛala ilyimiin

ilmadrasa (1)–ilbank (2)– ilfondo? (3)

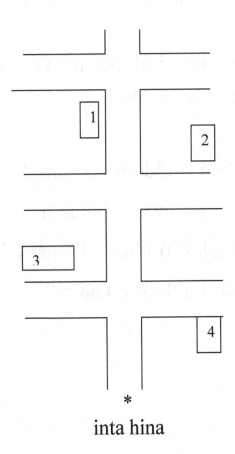

*
inta hina

<u>Drill 4:</u> Write the ordinal numbers in these sentences:

1- imši ɛalatuul wi baɛdeen xušš ...... šaariɛ yimiin.   (2)

2- xušš yimiin wi .... šaariɛ šimaal.   (1)

3- ana saakin fi .... beet fi iššaariɛ da.   (4)

4- maktab Mona .... maktab ɛala iššimaal.   (3)

5- huwwa saakin fi .... beet.   (5)

<u>Drill 5:</u> Answer the questions as in the example:

Ex: - inta saakin fi iddoor ikkaam *(what floor)*?   (5)
   -- iddoor ilxaamis.

1- hiyya sakna fi iddoor ikkaam ?   (3)

2- intu sakniin fi iddoor ikkaam ?   (7)

3- huwwa saakin fi iddoor ikkaam ?   (6)

4- inti sakna fi iddoor ikkaam ?   (1)

Listening:

Learn:
ilmabna : *the building*
door : *floor*
asanseer : *elevator*
amši izzaay : *How do I go?*

Listen to the dialogue and answer the questions:

1- Circle any word you recognize.
2- On what floor is Nagiib's office?
3- What is the direction of the office?

Dialogue B:

Raami : minfadlak, feen maktab ilostaaz Nagiib ?

ilmuwazzaf : huwwa fi ilmabna illi ɛala ilyimiin da.

Raami : huwwa fi iddoor ikkaam ?

ilmuwazzaf : fi iddoor issaabiɛ.

Raami : fiih asanseer ?

ilmuwazzaf : aywa, gamb ilbaab ɛala ilyimiin.

Raami : lamma atlaɛ min ilasanseer amši izzaay ?

ilmuwazzaf : xušš šimaal wi baɛdeen imši ɛalatuul, maktab ilostaaz Nagiib taalit maktab ɛala ilyimiin. ɛandak miɛaad ?

Raami : la'.

ilmuwazzaf : tayyib di?ii?a waHda ašuufu mawguud walla la'.

117

Lesson 11

ع and ilxodari

At the Greengrocer's!

Lesson Contents:

1- Question words *(How much?, What is the price?)*

2- Imperative *(give me)*

3- The verb "*to have*" *(he has, she has)*

4- Numbers 10-1000

Key Words

xodaar *vegetables*

batatis *potatoes*

tamatim *tomatoes*

kaam kiilo ?
How many kilos?

gineh /noss gineh /rob3 gineh
one pound/ ½ pound/ ¼ pound

Key words

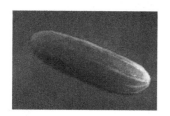
xiyaar
cucumber

gazar
carrot

koromb
cabbage

koosa
zucchini

filfil axdar
green pepper

besella
peas

bitingaan
eggplant

xass
lettuce

battiix
watermelon

ɛinab
grape

mooz
banana

toffaH
apple

DIALOGUE:

ɛand ilxodari ! *At the Greengrocer's!*

Linda   : sabaaH ilxeer! fiih bataatis kuwayyisa ?

ilxodari : aywa, bataatis momtaaza, ɛayza kaam kiilo ?

Linda   : iddiini itneen kiilo. ɛandak tamaatim ?

ilxodari : tabɛan, di tamaatim taaza.

Linda   : bikaam ikkiilo ?

ilxodari : itneen gineh.

Linda   : tayyib, ɛayza kiilo wi noss.

ilxodari : maaši, Haaga tanya ?

Linda   : la' xalaas, ɛaayiz kaam ?

Vocabulary

ilxodari	*greengrocer*
bataatis	*potatoes*
momtaaz /a	*excellent*
kaam kiilo	*how many kilos?*
iddiini	*give me (m., f.)*
tamaatim	*tomatoes*
tabɛan	*of course*
taaza	*fresh*
bikaam ?	*What is the price?*
noss	*half*
xalaas	*finished*

<u>Drill 1:</u> Answer the questions:

    1- Linda عayza eh ?

    2- hiyya عayza kaam kiilo bataatis ?

    3- ittamaatim taaza ?

    4- bikaam kiilo ittamaatim ?

    5- Linda عayza Haaga tanya ?

<u>Drill 2:</u> Choose the appropriate response:

1- bikaam kiilo ittamaatim ?   a- tabعan, di momtaaza.

2- عaayiz kaam kiilo ?   b- la', xalaas.

3- fiih bataatis ?   c- bi itneen gineh.

4- Haaga tanya ?   d- noss kiilo.

<u>Drill 3:</u> Right or wrong:

    1- Linda عayza mooz wi عinab.   ( )

    2- hiyya عayza kiilo wi noss tamaatim.   ( )

    3- fiih عand ilxodari bataatis wi tamaatim.   ( )

    4- ittmaatim bi talaata gineh.   ( )

    5- hiyya عayza itneen kiilo wi noss bataatis.   ( )

Grammar:

The Verb *"to have"*:

The verb *"to have"* in Arabic consists of the preposition (*"at"* **"ʕand"**) and an object pronoun. (Note: Object pronouns with prepositions are exactly like possessive pronouns).

Therefore, for **"huwwa** and **hiyya"**, the letters **"-u"** and **"-ha"** are suffixed to **"ʕand"** respectively.

- For *"she has"* there is an extra vowel appears **"a"** to avoid three consonants in a row.

Subject pronoun	Object Pronoun	ʕand *(at)*
ana	---i	ʕand<u>i</u>
inta	---ak	ʕand<u>ak</u>
inti	---ik	ʕand<u>ik</u>
huwwa	---u	ʕand<u>u</u>
hiyya	---ha	ʕand<u>aha</u> *

Negation:

- In Arabic the verb *"to have"* is negated with **"miš"**.

- huwwa miš ʕandu tamaatim.
He doesn't have tomatoes.

123

Imperative (Give Me):

m.	f.	pl,
--------	-------i	------u
iddii	iddi<u>i</u>	idd<u>u</u>	(give)

* iddi *(give)* + ni *(me)* ------------ iddiini

** *my* = i (ismi)   *me* = ni (iddiini)

kaam and bikaam?:

1- **kaam:** -It is used to ask the number of an item such as the building number.
-It uses the singular agreement of the noun, not the plural agreement like in English.

   kaam <u>kiilo</u> ?   *How many <u>kilos?</u>*

   -It could also be used to ask about the total price.

   ξaayiz kaam ?   *How much is the total price?*

2- **bikaam:** -It is used to ask about the price of an item.

   bikaam ilbataatis ?   *What is the price of potatoes?*

124

Numbers:

10 - ɛašara (١٠)   100 – miyya   (١٠٠)

20 – ɛišriin (٢٠)   200 – miteen   (٢٠٠)

30 – talatiin (٣٠)   300 – toltumiyya   (٣٠٠)

40 – arbiɛiin (٤٠)   400 – robɛumiyya (٤٠٠)

50 – xamsiin (٥٠)   500 – xomsumiyya (٥٠٠)

60 – sittiin (٦٠)   600 – sottumiyya   (٦٠٠)

70 – sabɛiin (٧٠)   700 – sobɛumiyya (٧٠٠)

80 – tamaniin(٨٠)   800 – tomnumiyya (٨٠٠)

90 – tesɛiin (٩٠)   900 – tosɛumiyya (٩٠٠)

100 – miyya (١٠٠)   1000 - alf   (١٠٠٠)

Drills

Drill 1: Do your shopping:

min fadlak – ع aayiz/a – ع andak

<u>xodaar</u> *(Vegetables)*

<u>fakha</u> *(Fruits)*

<u>Drill 2</u>: Fill the blanks with the appropriate suffix pronouns:

i, ak, ik, u, ha

1- inti ʕand… ʕarabiyya ?

2- madam Nadia ʕand…. agaaza bokra.

4- Hadritak ʕand…. awlaad ?

5- ana ʕand…. dars ʕarabi dilwa?ti.

6- AHmad ʕand…. šoghl *(work)* innaharda ?

<u>Drill 3</u>: Tell the price as indicated:

1- bikaam iššanta ?   (LE 150)

2- bikaam kiilo ilmooz ?   (LE 3)

3- bikaam ittarabeeza di ?   (LE500)

4- bikaam ilboluuza di ?   (LE 95)

5- bikaam kiilo issamak ?   (LE 23)

6- ʕaayiz kaam ?   (LE 18)

7- bikaam ittilifizyoon ?   (LE 899)

<u>Drill 4:</u> Reorder the words to make a sentence:

1- kiilo – wi – ɛaayiz – ɛinab – noss

2- besella – min fadlak – taaza – fiih – ?

3- kiilo – ɛaayiz – kaam – ?

4- axdar – ɛandak – filfil – ?

<u>Drill 5:</u> Translate into English:

1- ana ɛaayiz battiix kuwayyis wi aHmar.

2- huwwa ɛandu farawla taaza.

3- ilmooz axdar wi miš taaza.

4- iddiini kiilo wi noss ɛinab wi talaata kiilo toffaH.

5- fiih filfil axdar wi asfar.

6- la' miš ɛaayiz farawla, di ghaalia awi.

7- ɛayza kiilo bitingaan abyad wi koromba kibiira.

8- bikaam kiilo iggazar ?

128

Drill 6: Translate into Arabic:

1- I have a big car.

2- Do you (m.) have a pen?

3- She has a beautiful house.

4- They live in zamaalik.

5- She wants a hot coffee.

6- We are going to the Sheraton Hotel.

7- How much is the book?

8- My name is Linda ... and you (f.)?

9- How much is the bill?

10- Where is the bank?

11- This is my colleague (m.) Ahmed.

12- He is not well. He is a little tired.

13- Are you (pl.) from Canada?

14- The car is in front of the house.

15- Go straight ahead and then turn right.

16- Give me a kilo of tomatoes.

17- He doesn't have cabbage.

Listening:

Learn: suu? : *market*

ilasʕaar naar : *the prices are very high*

magnuuna : *crazy*

Listen to the dialogue and answer the questions:

1- Circle any word you recognize.
2- What vegetables did she buy?
3- What are the prices?

Dialogue B:

Samia : izzayyik ya Fariida, axbaarik eh ?

Fariida : ilHamdu lillah, gayya mineen ?

Samia : kont fi issuu?, asli ʕandi ʕozuuma innaharda.

Fariida : wi ilxodaar ʕaamil eh fi issuu? ?

Samia : wallahi ilxodaar Hilw bass ilasʕaar naar.

Fariida : leeh, gibti itamaatim bikaam ?

Samia : bi xamsa gineh.

Fariida : saHiiH illi ?aal ʕaleha magnuuna, tayyib wi ilbesella ?

Samia : ilbesella bi sabʕa, tisada?i ?

Fariida : aah momkin ʕašaan lissa gidiida, tayyib ana HaruuH wi ašuuf binafsi, bay bay !

Appendices
&
Glossary (English-Arabic)
&
Glossary (Arabic-English)

Appendix 1: Greetings

sabaaH ilxeer	*good morning*
sabaaH innuur	*good morning (response)*
masaa ilxeer	*good evening*
masaa innuur	*good evening (response)*
ahlan	*hello*
ahlan wa sahlan	*welcome*
ahlan biik/-i	*welcome (response)*
maɛa issalaama	*good bye*
allah yisallimak/-ik	*good bye (response)*
forsa saɛiida	*nice to meet you*
ana asɛad	*nice to meet you (response)*
issalamu ɛaleekum	*peace be upon you*
wi ɛaleekum issalaam	*and peace be upon you (response)*

Pronouns

ana	*I*
iHna	*we*
inta	*you (m.)*
inti	*you (f.)*
intu	*you(pl.)*
huwwa	*he*
hiyya	*she*
homma	*they*

Appendix 2:
Question words

eh	*what?*
izzaay	*how?*
miin	*who?*
feen	*where?*
mineen	*from where?*
kaam	*how many?/ how much?*
bikaam	*what is the price?*
imta	*when?*
fiih	*is there/ are there?*
leeh	*why?*
maɛa miin	*with whom?*
limiin	*for whom?*
bi eh	*by what?*
(any item) miin	*whose?*

Prepositions

fi	*in*
ɛala	*on*
gamb	*beside/ near/ next to*
maɛa	*with*
min	*from*
taHt	*under*
foo?	*over/ above*
gowwa	*inside*
barra	*outside*
been	*in between*
wara	*behind*
?oddaam	*in front of*

Appendix 3:
Adjectives

m. /f.

kuwayyis/a	*good*
taɛbaan/a	*tired*
saaʔiɛ/saʔɛa	*cold*
soxn/a	*hot*
kibiir/a	*big*
soghayyar/a	*small*
gidiid/a	*new*
ʔadiim/a	*old*
tawiil/a	*tall*
ʔosayyar/a	*short*
ghaali/a	*expensive*
rixiis/a	*cheap*
gamiil/a	*beautiful*
wiHiš/wiHša	*bad, ugly*

Colors:

m.	f.	
aHmar	Hamra	*red*
asfar	safra	*yellow*
axdar	xadra	*green*
azraʔ	zarʔa	*blue*
abyad	beeda	*white*
iswid	sooda	*black*
bonni		*brown*
romaadi		*grey*
bamba		*pink*
banafsigi		*purple*

Appendix 4:
Food Items:

šaay	*tea*
?ahwa (f.)	*coffee*
mayya (f.)	*water*
ɛasiir	*juice*
firaax (f.)	*chicken*
samak	*fish*
laHma (f.)	*meat*
salata (f.)	*salad*
šorba (f.)	*soup*
rozz	*rice*
makaroona (f.)	*macaroni*
beed	*eggs*
ɛeeš	*bread*
gibna (f.)	*cheese*
merabba (f.)	*jam*
zibda (f.)	*butter*

Fruits:

borto?aan	*orange*
farawla (f.)	*strawberry*
toffaH	*apple*
battiix	*watermelon*
ɛinab	*grape*
mooz	*banana*

Vegetables:

tamaatim (f.)	*tomatoes*
besella (f.)	*peas*
xiyaar	*cucumber*
gazar	*carrot*
xass	*lettuce*
koosa (f.)	*zucchini*
filfil axdar	*green pepper*
koromb	*cabbage*

Appendix 5:
Numbers:

1- waaHid	11- Hidaašar
2-itneen	12- itnaašar
3- talaata	13- talataašar
4- arbaεa	14- arbaεtašar
5- xamsa	15- xamastašar
6- sitta	16- sittašar
7- sabεa	17- sabaεtašar
8- tamanya	18- tamantašar
9- tesεa	19- tesaεtašar
10- εašara	20- εišriin

10- εašara	100- miyya
20- εišriin	200- miteen
30- talatiin	300- toltomiyya
40- arbiεiin	400- robεumiyya
50- xamsiin	500- xomsumiyya
60- sittiin	600- sottumiyya
70- sabεiin	700- sobεumiyya
80- tamaniin	800- tomnumiyya
90- tesεiin	900- tosεumiyya
100- miyya	1000- alf

Ordinal Numbers:

awwil	*first*	saatit- saadis	*sixth*
taani	*second*	saabiε	*seventh*
taalit	*third*	taamin	*eighth*
raabiε	*fourth*	taasiε	*ninth*
xaamis	*fifth*	εaašir	*tenth*

136

Appendix 6:
Days of the Week

issabt	*Saturday*
ilHadd	*Sunday*
ilitneen	*Monday*
ittalaat	*Tuesday*
ilarbaε	*Wednesday*
ilxamiis	*Thursday*
iggomεa	*Friday*

Months

yanaayir	*January*
febraayir	*February*
maaris	*March*
ibriil	*April*
maayu	*May*
yonyu	*June*
yolyu	*July*
aghostos	*August*
sebtamber	*September*
oktobar	*October*
nofamber	*November*
desamber	*December*

Glossary (English –Arabic)

A

a little bit	šiwayya
above	foo?
after noon	baɛd iddohr
after awhile	baɛd šiwayya
again (second time)	marra tanya
also	bardu
also	kamaan
America	Amriika (f.)
American (m., f.)	amriiki/-iyya
and	wi /wa
angry (m., f.)	zaɛlaan/a
any other service?	ayy xidma tanya
as	zayy
as you (m., f.)	zayyak/ik

B

bad- ugly(m., f.)	wiHiš/wiHša
bag	šanta (f.)
bathroom	Hammaam
beautiful (m., f.)	gamiil/a
behind	wara
below	taHt
beside	gamb
big (m., f.)	kibiir/a
bill	Hisaab
black (m., f.)	iswid / sooda
blue (m., f.)	azra? / zar?a

book	kitaab
boy	walad
bread	ɛeeš
breakfast	fitaar
bring (m., f., pl.)	haat/ i/ u
busy (m., f.)	mašghuul/a
but	bass
by the way	ɛala fikra

C

Cairo	ilqahira (f.)
Canada	Kanada (f.)
Canadian (m., f.)	kanadi/-iyya
can I help you?	ayy xidma
car	ɛarabiyya (f.)
chair	kursi
cheap (m., f.)	rixiis/a
cheese	gibna (f.)
chicken	firaax (f.)
children	awlaad
clean (m., f., pl.)	naddaf/ i/ u
clock	saaɛa (f.)
coffee	?ahwa (f.)
cold	bard
colleague (m, f.)	zimiil/ a
crazy (m., f.)	magnuun/a
cup	fingaan

D

day(s)	yoom (ayaam)
desk	maktab
dinner	ɛaša

director	modiir
door	baab
downstairs	taHt
downtown	west ilbalad
driver	sawwaa?

E

eggs	beed
Egypt	Masr (f.)
Egyptian (m., f.)	masri/-iyya
elevator	asanseer
embassy	sifaara (f.)
enter (m., f., pl.)	xušš/i/u
exactly	bizzabt
expensive (m., f.)	ghaali/a

F

few	šiwayya
fish	samak
food	akl
France	Faransa (f.)
French (m., f.)	faransi/-iyya
Friday	iggomɛa (f.)
friend (m., f.)	saaHib/ saHba
from	min
from where?	mineen
fruits	fakha (f.)

G

Germany	Almaania (f.)
get in (m., f., pl.)	itfaddal/i/u
girl	bint (f.)
glass	kobbaaya (f.)

go (m., f., pl.)	imši/i/u
God be praised	ilHamdu lillah
going (m., f., pl.)	raayiH /rayHa /-iin
good (m., f.)	kuwayyis /-a
good evening	masaa ilxeer
good evening (response)	masaa innuur
good morning	sabaaH ilxeer
good morning (response)	sabaaH innuur
green (m., f.)	axdar / xadra
guard (m., f.)	bawwaab/a

H

happy (m., f.)	mabsuut/-a
he	huwwa
he has	ʕandu
hello	ahlan
here	hina
hot (m., f.)	soxn/ a
hotel	fondo?
house	beet
how are you (m., f.)?	izzayyak /-ik
how many?	kaam
how many kilos?	kaam kiilo
how much?	kaam
husband	gooz

I

I	ana
I am sorry (m., f.)	aasif / asfa
I have	ʕandi
I will see you (m., f.)	ašuufak/-ik
If God wills	inša' allah

in	fi
in between	been
in front of	?oddaam
in the evening	billeel
Italy	Itaalia (f.)

J

jam	merabba (f.)
juice	ɛasiir

L

leave (m., f., pl.)	imši/i/u
lemon	lamoon
lesson	dars
let us go	yalla biina.
like	zayy
like you (m., f.)	zayyak/ik
little bit	šiwayya
living (m., f., pl.)	saakin /sakna/-iin
living (in country) (m., f., pl.)	ɛaayiš /ɛayša/-iin
look (m., f.)	šuuf/i
lunch	ghada

M

macaroni	makaroona (f.)
man	raagil
mango	manga (f.)
market	suu?
maybe	yimkin
meat	laHma (f.)
meeting	igtimaaɛ
Miss	aanesa (f.)
Monday	ilitneen

money	filuus (f.)
month(s)	šahr (šuhuur)
morning	sobH
Mr.	ostaaz
Mrs.	madam (f.)
my colleague (m, f.)	zimiili/ zimiilti
my name	ismi
my wife	miraati (f.)

N

name	ism
new (m., f.)	gidiid/a
news	axbaar
newspaper	gornaan
next street	iššaariɛ iggay
nice to meet you	forsa saɛiida
nice to meet you (response)	ana asɛad
nine	tesɛa
no	la'
noon	iddohr
not	miš
nothing	mafiiš Haaga
number	nimra (f.)

O

O, vocative particle	ya
office	maktab
OK!	tayyib / maaši/ Haadir
old (m., f.)	?adiim/a
on	ɛala
or	walla
orange	borto?aan

143

over	foo?

P

party	Hafla (f.)
Pen	?alam
picture	suura (f.)
please (m., f.)	min fadlak/ik
professor	ostaaz
purse	šanta (f.)

R

red (m., f.)	aHmar / Hamra
restaurant	matɛam
rice	rozz
right	yimiin

S

sad (m., f.)	zaɛlaan/ a
salad	salata (f.)
Saturday	issabt
Saudi Arabia	Issoɛodiyya (f.)
school	madrasa (f.)
she	hiyya
she has	ɛandaha
shoes	gazma (f.)
short (m., f.)	?osayyar/a
sister	oxt
small (m., f.)	soghayyar/a
soft drink	Haaga sa?ɛa (f.)
soup	šorba (f.)
straight ahead	ɛalatuul
strawberry	farawla (f.)
street	šaariɛ

summer	seef
Sunday	ilHad

T

T.V.	tilifizyoon
table	tarabeeza (f.)
tall (m., f.)	tawiil/a
taxi	taksi
tea	šaay
telephone	tilifoon
thanks	šokran
that (m., f.)	da/di
there are	fiih
there is	fiih
they	homma
this (m., f.)	da/di
Thursday	ilxamiis
tired (m., f.)	taεbaan/a
today	innaharda
tomorrow	bokra
Tuesday	ittalaat
two	itneen

U

under	taHt
upset (m., f.)	zaεlaan/ a

V

vegetables	xodaar
very	awi

W

walk (m., f., pl.)	imši/i/u
wanting (m., f., pl.)	εaayiz /εayza/-iin

watch	saaɛa (f.)
water	mayya (f.)
we	iHna
Wednesday	ilarbaɛ
week (s)	isbuuɛ (asaabiɛ)
welcome	ahlan wa sahlan
welcome (m., f.) (response)	ahlan biik/-i
well (m., f.)	kuwayyis /-a
what?	eh
what number?	kaam
what time is it?	issaaɛa kaam
where?	feen
white	abyad / beeda
who?	miin
why?	leeh
wife of	miraat
with	maɛa
woman	sitt (f.)

Y

year (s)	sana (siniin)
yellow (m., f.)	asfar / safra
yes	aywa
yesterday	imbaariH
you (m., f. (for respect))	Hadritak/-ik
you (m., f.)	inta/inti
you (pl.)	intu
you are welcome	ilɛafwu
you have (m., f.)	ɛandak/-ik
your name (m., f.)	ismak/-ik

Glossary (Arabic – English)

A

aanesa (f.)	*Miss*
aasif	*I am sorry (m.)*
abyad / beeda	*white (m., f.)*
ahlan	*hello*
ahlan biik/-i	*welcome (response) (m., f.)*
ahlan wa sahlan	*welcome*
aHmar / Hamra	*red*
akl	*food*
almaania (f.)	*Germany*
amriika (f.)	*America*
amriiki/-iyya	*American (m., f.)*
ana asɛad	*nice to meet you (response)*
ana	*I*
asanseer	*elevator*
asfa (f.)	*I am sorry (f.)*
asfar / safra	*yellow (m., f.)*
ašuufak/-ik	*I will see you (m., f.)*
awi	*very*
awlaad	*children*
axbaar (f.)	*news*
axdar / xadra	*green (m., f.)*
aywa	*yes*
ayy xidma	*can I help you?*
ayy xidma tanya	*any other service?*
azra? / zar?a	*blue (m., f.)*

B

baɛd iddohr	*after noon*

baʕd šiwayya	*after awhile*
baab	*door*
bard	*cold*
bardu	*also*
bass	*but*
bawwaab/ a	*guard (m., f.)*
beed	*eggs*
been	*in between*
beet	*house*
billeel	*in the evening*
bint (f.)	*girl*
bizzabt	*exactly*
bokra	*tomorrow*
borto?aan	*orange*

D

da	*this /that (m.)*
dars	*lesson*
di	*this /that (f.)*

E

eh	*what?*

F

fakha (f.)	*fruits*
Faransa (f.)	*France*
faransi/-iyya	*French (m., f.)*
farawla (f.)	*straw berry*
feen	*where?*
fi	*in*
fiih	*there is/ there are*
filuus (f.)	*money*
fingaan	*cup*

148

firaax (f.)	*chicken*
fitaar	*breakfast*
fondo?	*hotel*
foo?	*above/ over/ upstairs*
forsa saɛiida	*nice to meet you*
G	
gamb	*beside*
gamiil/a	*beautiful (m., f.)*
gazma (f.)	*shoes*
ghaali/a	*expensive (m., f.)*
ghada	*lunch*
gibna (f.)	*cheese*
gidiid/a	*new (m., f.)*
gooz	*husband*
gornaan	*newspaper*
h	
haat/i/u	*bring (imp.)(m., f., pl.)*
hina	*here*
hiyya (f.)	*she*
homma	*they*
huwwa	*he*
H	
Haadir	*ok*
Haaga sa?ɛa (f.)	*soft drink*
Hadritak/-ik	*you (m., f. (for respect))*
Hafla (f.)	*party*
Hammaam	*bathroom*
Hisaab	*bill*
I	
iddohr	*noon*

iggomɛa (f.)	Friday
igtimaaɛ	meeting
iHna	we
ilarbaɛ	Wednesday
ilɛafwu	you are welcome
ilHad	Sunday
ilHamdu lillah	God be praised
ilitneen	Monday
ilqahira (f.)	Cairo
ilxamiis	Thursday
imbaariH	yesterday
imši/i/u	go/ walk (m., f., pl.)
innaharda	today
inša' allah	If God wills
inta	you (m.)
inti (f.)	you (f.)
intu	you (pl.)
isbuu ɛ (asaabiɛ)	week (s)
ism	name
ismi	my name
ismak/-ik	your name (m., f.)
issaaɛa kaam	what time is it?
issabt	Saturday
issoɛodiyya (f.)	Saudi Arabia
issobH	in the morning
iswid / soda	black(m., f.)
iššaariɛ iggay	next street (the coming street)
itaalia (f.)	Italy
itfaddal/i/u	get in (m., f., pl.)
itneen	two
ittalaat	Tuesday

izzayyak /-ik	*how are you (m., f.)?*

K

kaam	*how many?/ how much? (what number?)*
kaam kiilo	*how many kilos?*
kamaan	*also*
kanadi/-iyya	*Canadian (m., f.)*
kibiir/a	*big (m., f.)*
kitaab	*book*
kobbaaya (f.)	*glass*
kursi	*chair*
kuwayyis /-a	*well / good (m., f.)*

L

la'	*no*
laHma (f.)	*meat*
lamoon	*lemon*
leeh	*why?*

M

mabsuut/-a	*happy (m., f.)*
madam (f.)	*Mrs.*
madrasa (f.)	*school*
mafiiš Haaga	*nothing (lit.: there is not anything)*
magnuun/a	*crazy (m., f.)*
makaroona (f.)	*macaroni*
maktab	*office, desk*
manga (f.)	*mango*
marra tanya	*again (second time)*
masaa ilxeer	*Good evening*
masaa innuur	*Good evening (response)*
masr (f.)	*Egypt*
masri/-iyya	*Egyptian (m., f.)*

mašghuul/ a	*busy (m., f.)*
matɛam	*restaurant*
maɛa	*with*
mayya (f.)	*water*
merabba (f.)	*jam*
miin	*who?*
min fadlak/ik	*please (m., f.)*
min	*from*
mineen	*from where (where ...from)*
miraat	*wife of*
miraati (f.)	*my wife*
miš	*not*
modiir	*director*

N

naddaf/i/u	*clean (imp.) (m., f., pl.)*
nimra (f.)	*number*

O

ostaaz /a	*Mr. / professor (m., f.)*
oxt	*sister*

R

raagil	*man*
raayiH /rayHa /-iin	*going (m., f., pl.)*
rixiis/a	*cheap (m., f.)*
rozz	*rice*

S

saaHib/ saHba	*friend (m., f.)*
saaɛa (f.)	*watch, clock*
saakin /sakna/-iin	*living (m., f., pl.)*
sabaaH ilxeer	*Good morning*
sabaaH innuur	*Good morning (response)*

salata (f.)	*salad*
samak	*fish*
sana (siniin)	*year (s)*
sawwaaʔ	*driver*
seef	*summer*
sifaara (f.)	*embassy*
sitt (f.)	*woman*
soghayyar/a	*small (m., f.)*
soxn/ a	*hot (m., f.)*
suura (f.)	*picture*
suuʔ	*market*

š

šaariɛ	*street*
šaay	*tea*
šahr (šuhuur)	*month(s)*
šanta (f.)	*bag, purse*
šiwayya (f.)	*a little bit / few*
šokran	*thanks*
šorba (f.)	*soup*
šuuf/i	*look (m., f.)*

T

taɛbaan/a	*tired (m., f.)*
taHt	*under/ below/ downstairs*
taksi	*taxi*
tarabeeza (f.)	*table*
tawiil/a	*tall (m., f.)*
tayyib	*OK!*
tesɛa	*nine*
tilifizyoon	*T.V.*
tilifoon	*telephone*

W

walad	*boy*
walla	*or*
wara	*behind*
west ilbalad	*downtown*
wi/ wa	*and*
wiHiš	*bad- ugly(m.)*
wiHša	*bad- ugly(f.)*

X

xodaar	*vegetables*
xušš/i/u	*enter (m., f., pl.)*

Y

ya	*O, vocative particle*
yalla biina.	*let us go*
yimiin	*right*
yimkin	*maybe*
yoom (ayaam)	*day(s)*

Z

zaʕlaan/ a	*sad, upset, angry*
zayyak	*as/like you*
zimiil/a	*colleague (m, f.)*
zimiili/ zimiilti	*my colleague (m, f.)*

?

?adiim/a	*old (m., f.)*
?ahwa (f.)	*coffee*
?alam	*pen*
?oddaam	*in front of*
?osayyar/a	*short (m., f.)*

ع

ʕaayiš /ʕayša/-iin	*living (in country)(m., f., pl.)*

ʕaayiz /ʕayza/-iin	*wanting (m., f., pl.)*
ʕalatuul	*straight ahead*
ʕala	*on*
ʕala fikra	*by the way*
ʕandaha	*she has*
ʕandak	*you(m.) have*
ʕandi	*I have*
ʕandik	*you (f.) have*
ʕandu	*he has*
ʕarabiyya (f.)	*car*
ʕasiir	*juice*
ʕaša	*dinner*
ʕeeš	*bread*